Come to
EASTER

Come to EASTER

The
CUSTOMS
of the
LENTEN &
EASTER
SEASONS

Compiled by Pat Floyd

Abingdon Press

Come to Easter:
The Customs of the Lenten and Easter Seasons

ISBN 0-687-05634-9

Layout and design by John Boegel

MANUFACTURED IN THE UNITED STATES OF AMERICA
98 99 00 01 02 03 04 05 06 07 — 10 9 8 7 6 5 4 3 2 1

CONTENTS

JUST BEFORE LENT

*T*n earlier times Lent was a solemn season. People ate no meat, fish, cheese, butter, eggs, or milk and used no lard in cooking. Until 1863 England had a law forbidding these foods during Lent. Violators could be fined or imprisoned. Only the sick and infirm were excused. Brightly colored clothes, games, parties, and festivities were forbidden. But the days just before Lent were another matter!

MARDI GRAS

For many European countries the time before Lent was carnival time with parades, dances, games, sports, antics, and wild revels. *Mardi Gras*, literally fat Tuesday, was a feast day before Ash Wednesday. Now Mardi Gras is a pre-lenten carnival celebrated in parts of Europe, Latin America, and North America. New Orleans is famous for its Mardi Gras: Just after Epiphany, January 6, festivities begin with balls and parades and continue until the early hours of Ash Wednesday morning.

SHROVETIDE

Shrovetide is the English name for the three or four days before Lent. The name comes from the word *shrive*, to confess one's sins and receive absolution. Christians were expected to prepare for Lent by being shriven. But Shrovetide was also a time to clear the house of foods forbidden during Lent.

COLLOP MONDAY AND SHROVE TUESDAY

n Collop Monday small pieces, or collops, of meat were eaten. On Shrove Tuesday pancake meals and pancake contests used up butter, eggs, and milk. In an Olney, England, custom started in 1445, women raced from the town square to the church. Each carried a frying pan and had to flip a pancake three times as she ran. Pancake Day is still observed in many places. Why not celebrate with a pancake meal in your church or home? Or follow the Pennsylvania Dutch *Fastnacht Eve* custom and serve doughnuts instead.

CLEAN MONDAY

Spring house cleaning is an ancient—and modern—Lenten tradition. In Russia Clean Monday, cleaning on the Monday before Ash Wednesday, was the custom. Pans were scoured to remove any lingering hint of forbidden meat fat. In some rural areas of the United States, people cleaned the church on the Monday of Holy Week.

LENT

*L*ent begins on Ash Wednesday and ends on the Saturday before Easter. The word Lent comes from the Anglo-Saxon word *lencten,* which means "spring," the time of the lengthening of days. Lent lasts forty days, not counting Sundays.

WHY FORTY DAYS?

*J*esus was in the wilderness forty days facing temptation and discerning the kind of ministry God intended for him (Matthew 4:1-11; Mark 1:12-13; Luke 4:1-13). In Scripture forty days or forty years is often the duration of a time of punishment, repentance, fasting, or vigil: The children of Israel were in the wilderness forty years; Jonah preached that Nineveh would be destroyed in forty days; Acts 1:3 reports that the risen Christ appeared to his followers for forty days before his ascension.

WHY NOT COUNT SUNDAYS?

In the first century an epistle attributed to Barnabas says, "We keep with joy the day on which Jesus rose from the dead." In the second century Justin Martyr wrote, "We all gather on Sunday because on the first day . . . Jesus Christ our Savior rose from the dead." Sunday is always a celebration of Jesus' victory over sin and death. Even during Lent, Sunday is a "little Easter."

COLOR FOR LENT

Purple, a royal color that also signifies penitence and preparation, is used during Lent on cloths for altar, pulpit, and lectern and on stoles and banners.

ASH WEDNESDAY

*T*he date of Ash Wednesday, determined by the date of Easter, may fall anytime from February 3 to March 10. Ash Wednesday begins the season of Lent with worship that focuses on the themes of sin and death in the light of God's redeeming love in Jesus Christ. Traditional words used during the service are "Remember that you are dust, and to dust you shall return." We receive everlasting life only as a gift of God's grace.

Ash Wednesday worship, whether with a congregation or alone, is a call to observe Lent as a time of self-examination and repentance, of prayer and self-denial, of reading and Bible study, of meditation on Jesus' life and death, and of giving oneself to others, especially those who suffer and are in need.

SIGNIFICANCE OF ASHES

 Scripture has many references to ashes used as a sign of mortality and of repentance. Abraham spoke of himself as being "but dust and ashes" (Genesis 18:27). After Job lost everything, he sat among the ashes (Job 2:8). The king, the people, and even the animals of Nineveh donned sackcloth and ashes as a sign of repentance (Jonah 3:5-10), and Jesus spoke of cities repenting in sackcloth and ashes (Luke 10:13).

In many churches palms used on Palm Sunday the previous year are burned and mixed with a little water to make ashes for Ash Wednesday. Sometimes persons write a particular sin or wrong or something they want God's help in overcoming to be burned with the palms. In the service the pastor uses the ashes to make a cross on the forehead of each worshiper.

THE MEANING OF LENT FOR US

*I*n our busy, secular world, we all need times of reflection and renewal. Lent can be such a time. Lent is above all a time to remember Jesus, to walk with him in study, prayer, and service to others, a time to engage in personal and family worship. Yet in order to be the body of Christ, Christians need to come together to worship and study with others—on Ash Wednesday, on Sundays, and at special services during Lent and Holy Week. Lent is a time for congregational worship.

GIVING UP AND ADDING ON

Giving up something for Lent is a tradition that probably grows out of the history of Lenten penance and fasting. Most of us have things in our lives that we need to give up permanently. Lent is a good time to begin. Or we might give up something we value in order to identify with what Jesus gave for us or in order to help people in need. Churches or individuals may make an offering of money saved from the practice of delf-denial to give to people in need. We may want to add some things for Lent—acts of kindness, generosity, compassion, and love.

WATCH FOR SIGNS OF SPRING

*W*here seasons change, a real joy of the Lenten season is watching for signs of spring and new life. The days get noticeably longer. In northern regions snow melts; streams and icicles thaw. Migrating birds begin to return. Crocuses may bloom while vestiges of snow still remain. Leaf buds swell and yellow-green leaves appear on the willows. Families can enjoy keeping a record of the changes they see.

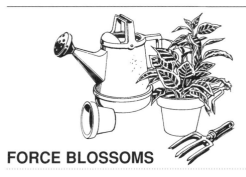

FORCE BLOSSOMS

Cut twigs of any tree with swollen leaf buds or branches of fruit trees or forsythia and place them in water in a sunny window and watch leaves or flowers appear.

POT BULBS

Plant paper white narcissus bulbs in a shallow bowl of small stones and fill with water to the level of the stones. Put in a dark place until rootlets begin to appear, then bring to a bright or sunny place. Keep water to the base of the bulbs.

MAKE AN EGG-SHELL GARDEN

*F*ill halves of egg shells with potting soil, sprinkle with grass seeds, and water. Place the shells in egg cups or an egg carton and watch the bright green of new grass appear.

ENJOY SPECIAL FOODS

Hot cross buns, first served on Good Friday, are now eaten throughout Lent. Use roll mix for buns adding 1/2 cup raisins and 1 teaspoon of grated orange rind. Bake and cool, then frost with a cross of icing.

PRETZELS

*R*oman Christians made pretzels from flour, salt, and water to eat on fast days. They called them *bracellae*, little arms, because the shape looked like arms crossed in prayer. The three sections of the pretzel reminded of the Trinity. Germans called them *brezeln*, the word from which our word pretzel comes. Pretzels were made and eaten throughout Lent.

3 cups warm milk
1 pkg. dry yeast
1 tsp. salt
1 Tbsp. sugar
1/4 cup melted shortening
7 cups flour
1 egg white
coarse salt

Add yeast to a half cup of the warm milk and stir until dissolved. Add salt, sugar, shortening, and flour and mix well. Knead six to eight minutes until smooth, adding flour if necessary. Place in a bowl, cover, and let rise about an hour until doubled. Punch down and let rest 10 minutes. With floured hands, roll a golf-ball-size piece of dough to a 14-to-16 inch roll. On a cookie sheet form a pretzel shape, crossing the ends of the roll to look like arms crossed in prayer. Keep pretzels apart. Brush with egg white mixed with a little water. Sprinkle with coarse salt. Let rise 30 minutes. Bake at 400° for 15 minutes. Makes about three dozen.

HOLY WEEK

*H*oly Week is the time when Christians re-live the events of Jesus' last week on earth: his triumphal entry into Jerusalem, cleansing the Temple, teaching his followers, dealing with challenges of Pharisees and Sadducees, his Last Supper with the disciples, prayer in the Garden of Gethsemane, betrayal, trial, crucifixion, death, and burial. Holy Week is a time to join with others to worship and remember.

PALM/PASSION SUNDAY

On Palm/Passion Sunday, the Sunday before Easter, worship services celebrate Jesus' entry into Jerusalem amidst the joyful welcome of his followers, but they also deal with the story of his passion and death. Sometimes the service begins with a procession carrying palms or other leafy branches. Each worshiper may be given a small cross made of palm leaves to wear.

TO HONOR KINGS

Several Old Testament scripture passages tell about processions to honor kings. Matthew and John quote Zechariah's prophecy of God's victory (9:9):

Rejoice greatly,
   O daughter Zion!
Shout aloud,
   O daughter Jerusalem!
Lo, your king comes to you;
   triumphant and victorious
      is he,
humble and riding on a
   donkey.

MAUNDY THURSDAY

On Thursday of Holy Week Christians commemorate Jesus' Last Supper when he broke bread and gave the cup to his disciples, initiating the Sacrament of the Lord's Supper. John's Gospel tells of Jesus washing disciples feet and giving them a new commandment. Our Maundy Thursday worship includes Holy Communion and sometimes foot washing as well.

Maundy Thursday takes its name from the Latin word for commandment, *mandatum*. At the Last Supper Jesus said, "I

give you a new commandment, that you love one another. Just as I have loved you, you also should love one another" (John 13:34). This day is also called Holy Thursday.

GOOD FRIDAY

On the day commemorating Jesus' death on the cross many churches have three-hour services from noon to three focusing on Jesus' words from the cross. Others have evening services. Good Friday may once have been God's Friday because Jesus' death shows God's love and salvation offered the world.

THE GREAT THREE DAYS

*T*he Great Three Days, sunset on Holy Thursday through sunset on Easter Day, are the climax of Lent and of the Christian year. These days proclaim the paschal mystery, the saving events of Jesus' suffering, death, and resurrection. Maundy Thursday and Good Friday services may be connected by a prayer vigil that lasts through Holy Saturday (when Jesus lay in the tomb) until the first service of Easter.

TENEBRAE

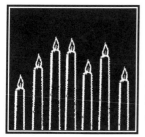

Following Communion on Holy Thursday or on Good Friday evening some churches have a service of Tenebrae or "Darkness," which originated in the twelfth century. As Jesus' sufferings are recalled from betrayal to burial in the tomb, candles are extinguished, one by one, until the room is left in darkness.

THE PASCHAL OR EASTER VIGIL

In the earliest centuries the events of Holy Week were celebrated in a single service, a vigil that began on Saturday night and continued until Easter dawn. It celebrated with joy the history of Christ's saving work and was a time to baptize converts and to greet the first moments of Easter Day.

Easter

"On the first day of the week, at early dawn, they came to the tomb, taking the spices that they had prepared" (Luke 24:1-2).

· · · · ·

"Why do you look for the living among the dead? He is not here, but has risen" (Luke 24:5).

· · · · ·

"They were saying, 'The Lord has risen indeed, and he has appeared to Simon!'" (Luke 24:34).

· · · · ·

"Jesus said to her, 'Mary!' She turned and said to him in Hebrew, 'Rabbouni!' (which means Teacher)" (John 20:16).

· · · · ·

"Jesus came and stood among them and said, 'Peace be with you'" (John 20:19).

*E*aster was a great surprise to Jesus' followers. Ancient manuscripts of Mark end with 16:8, "Terror and amazement had seized them; and they said nothing to anyone, for they were afraid." In our world cruel executions don't become joyous resurrections except by the power of God. But the presence and power of the risen Christ among his followers soon led them to tell the world, "Christ is risen! He is risen indeed!" Alleluia, which means "Praise ye the Lord!" is our response to what God has done.

SUNRISE SERVICES

Like the women who came to the tomb at dawn, many churches have sunrise services as the first service of Easter. A widespread belief once held that the sun danced for joy on Easter morning. The sunrise is a symbol of Jesus' resurrection.

NAMES FOR EASTER

*T*he word paschal (pertaining to Easter or Passover) is from *pesah* the Hebrew word for Passover. In several languages the word for Easter comes from the same root: *Pâques* in French, *Pascua de Resurrección* in Spanish, *Pasqua* in Italian, and *pask* in Swedish. In the eighth century, Venerable Bede wrote that the English word *Easter* came from Eastre, the Anglo-Saxon goddess whose holiday was on the spring equinox, March 21.

EASTER COLORS AND CANDLE

White and gold are joyous and festive colors to use at Easter and throughout the Easter season on cloths for altar, pulpit, and lectern and on stoles and banners. A large white candle called a paschal candle may be used every Sunday during the Easter Season.

DATE OF EASTER

*T*he date for celebrating Easter was agreed on in the west only after centuries of discussion and debate. Easter Sunday is the first Sunday after the full moon that occurs on or next after March 21, the spring equinox. Thus, Easter can be any time from March 22 through April 25. Orthodox Churches set the date of Easter by a different system.

SYMBOLS OF RESURRECTION

A symbol is a visible sign of something that is invisible. Christian art uses a variety of symbols to represent Jesus' resurrection and our hope of resurrection.

Empty cross. The cross is empty because Jesus rose from the dead.

Empty tomb. Jesus defeated the power of death and left the tomb.

Lily and bulb. A green and flowering plant grows from a bulb that seems lifeless.

Peacock. Every year the peacock sheds and regrows his splendid tail feathers.

Butterfly and cocoon. Out of a seemingly lifeless cocoon, a caterpillar is transformed into a butterfly.

Phoenix or fire bird. This mythical bird was said to rise from the ashes of fire that burned its old body.

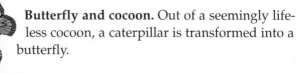

EASTER CUSTOMS: BUNNIES AND BONNETS

*F*rom ancient times, Christians have adopted symbols and customs of the world around them and invested them with Christian meaning. Such has been the case with Easter customs.

THE EASTER BUNNY

In ancient Egypt the hare was a symbol of the full moon, which falls near Easter. The hare and the full moon were also associated with the goddess Eastre. The many baby hares born in spring also suggested new life. Where rabbits were better known than the larger hare, the rabbit or bunny became an Easter symbol. In Germany the Easter bunny was first reputed to bring colored eggs to children on Easter morning. Children made nests of grass for the bunny to fill with colored eggs. Easter baskets have replaced nests.

EASTER BONNETS

Until the eighteenth century, Easter came near New Year's Day. (March 25 in the Julian calendar. Our Gregorian calendar wasn't adopted in America until 1752.) New clothes were considered good luck for the New Year and a sign of new life in Christ at Easter. New Year's Day on January 1 didn't change the custom of new clothes for Easter, and hats or bonnets were especially prized.

EASTER CUSTOMS: CHICKS AND EGGS

Easter Eggs

When eating eggs was forbidden during Lent, eggs were an especially welcome treat at Easter. In many countries eggs were given as Easter gifts. In 1290, King Edward I of England had 450 eggs dyed and gave one as a gift to each of his servants. In Russia eggs were dyed a deep red to suggest the blood of Christ. Pysanki (pee SANK ee) eggs from Poland and the Ukraine are decorated with elaborate designs that take hours or days to make.

Baby Chicks
Like baby rabbits born at Easter time, baby chicks also suggest new life. The mystery of a bird or a chicken coming out of a lifeless-looking egg shell suggests Jesus' resurrection from the tomb.

Egg Hunts and Egg Rolls
Easter eggs have been used in many kinds of games. Most widespread is the Easter egg hunt. The Easter bunny or adults hide eggs for children to find. Egg rolling started in Britain in the 19th century. The object is to see whose egg will roll down a hill first without breaking. Dolly Madison started egg rolling for children on the Capitol Hill lawn in 1809. In 1870 Rutherford B. Hayes moved the event to the White House lawn.

TO MAKE FOR EASTER

Dyed Eggs

*H*ard boiled eggs may be colored with commercial dye or with food color and a teaspoon of vinegar added to a cup of hot water. Use natural materials to color eggs as people did before commercial dyes were available. For yellow eggs, place dry skins of onions in cold water and boil five to ten minutes. Strain the dye and add 1 tablespoon of vinegar. Prepared in the same way, beet juice will make a pink dye, spinach green, and tea tan. Natural dyes usually make soft pastel shades rather than deep hues. Experiment with a variety of materials.

To hollow out eggs:
Let eggs sit at room temperature for two or three hours. Shake each egg. Punch a hole in the larger end of the egg and enlarge the hole slightly. Punch another hole in the small end, and blow the egg out through the larger hole. Wash out the shells and dye.

An Easter Egg Tree
Cut an interestingly shaped bare branch, place it in a pot, and anchor it firmly with dirt or stones. Decorate the branch with hollowed-out dyed eggs. Tie narrow ribbon around each egg and tie to the branch or tape cord to the eggs and tie to the branch. Cord could be threaded through the holes in the egg with a very long needle.

MORAVIAN EASTER CELEBRATIONS

*A*t a time when Puritans frowned on Christmas and Easter celebration, the Moravians brought their customs to Pennsylvania and North Carolina. At Easter there was the love feast: Saturday afternoon worship with trombone choir, midnight worship with house-to-house singing until dawn, a walk to the cemetery to see the rising sun and to hear glorious singing, and breakfast of coffee and sugar-cake.

Moravian Love Feast Buns
1 package yeast
1/4 cup tepid water
1 cup sugar
1 egg, beaten
1/4 cup soft butter melted butter for
    glazing
1 tsp. salt
1/4 cup warm mashed potatoes
7-8 cups flour
2 cups lukewarm water
melted butter

Dissolve yeast in 1/4 cup tepid water. Add sugar to beaten egg; then add soft butter, salt, warm potatoes, and yeast mixture. Add flour and warm water alternately to make a soft but firm dough. On a lightly floured surface, knead until smooth. Cover with a warm cloth and set in a warm place to rise. When dough is double in size, punch it down and make into buns 3" to 4" in diameter. Place on a cookie sheet and bake in 400° oven about 20 minutes. Brush with melted butter. Makes 18-20 buns.

Easter Lilies
All flowers speak of the joy of Easter, but the white, trumpet-shaped Bermuda lily with its fragrance and beauty says to us "Easter."

Easter Monday
Where Easter Monday was a holiday, it was sometimes celebrated with games, joke-telling, boisterous fun, and Easter egg hunts.

THE EASTER SEASON

*T*he Easter Season, also known as the Great Fifty Days, begins at sunset on Easter Eve and continues through the Day of Pentecost. This is a season for celebrating with joy Christ's resurrection and ascension and the giving of the Holy Spirit on the first Easter (John 20:22-23) and on the Day of Pentecost (Acts 2).

· · · · ·

Ascension Day, when Jesus ascended to heaven, is the fortieth day after Easter.

· · · · ·

Pentecost, the fiftieth day after Easter, comes from the Greek word for fiftieth, *pentekoste*. Greek-speaking Jews called the Jewish Feast of Weeks the Day of Pentecost. Acts 2 tells how the anxious and fearful disciples, who had gathered on the Day of Pentecost, were filled with the Holy Spirit and thereafter preached boldly the gospel of Jesus Christ.

A Living Presence

*E*aster season reminds us that Jesus said, "I am with you always, to the end of the age" (Matthew 28:20). The risen Christ is with us every day: when we pray, when we make decisions, when we say grace at meals, when we work and play, when we are anxious or afraid, when we are joyful, when we are thankful, and when we give and receive love.

Remember the traditional Easter greeting:

He is risen!
He is risen indeed!

Notes and Ideas for Your Family Celebrations